A CENTURY
of IMMIGRATION

1820–1924

★ ★ *The Drama of* AMERICAN HISTORY ★ ★

A CENTURY
of IMMIGRATION

1820–1924

Christopher Collier
James Lincoln Collier

BENCHMARK BOOKS

MARSHALL CAVENDISH
NEW YORK

ACKNOWLEDGMENT: The authors wish to thank Bruce M. Stave, Professor of History, University of Connecticut, for his careful reading of the text of this volume of The Drama of American History and his thoughtful and useful comments. The work has been much improved by Professor Stave's notes. The authors are deeply in his debt, but, of course, assume full responsibility for the substance of the work, including any errors that may appear.

New York was the principal port of entry for European immigration, and in 1855 the state set up a reception center at Castle Garden on the tip of Manhattan where new arrivals spent a few hours or a day bathing, eating, and answering questions of officials who also provided information about jobs, lodgings, and money changing. In 1890 the U.S. government took over those functions and established a more elaborate center on Ellis Island in New York Harbor in sight of the Statue of Liberty with its inscription: "Give me your tired, your poor, Your huddled masses yearning to breathe free, The wretched refuse of your teeming shore. Send these, the homeless, tempest-tost to me, I lift my lamp beside the golden door." By the time it was closed in 1954, over 16 million people had come to the United States through Ellis Island. Today it is a museum of immigration history.

Photo research by James Lincoln Collier.
COVER PHOTO: Museum of the City of New York
PICTURE CREDITS: The photographs in this book are used by permission and through the courtesy of :
Jamestown-Yorktown Educational Trust: 10. Joslyn Art Museum, Omaha, Nebraska: 12. Museum of the City of New York: 14, 21, 32, 34, 35, 47, 48, 49. Corbis-Bettmann: 19 (top), 19 (bottom), 28 (right), 28 (left), 31, 43, 55, 56, 58, 59, 76, 84. New York Public Library: 26, 39 (left), 39 (right), 45, 63 (left), 63 (right), 70, 75. Library of Congress: 71.
Independence National Historic Park: 81 (top), 81 (bottom), 82.

Benchmark Books
Marshall Cavendish Corporation
99 White Plains Road
Tarrytown, New York 10591-9001

Library of Congress Cataloging-in-Publication Data

Collier, Christopher, date
A century of immigration : 1820 –1924 / by Christopher Collier, James Lincoln Collier.
p. cm. — (The drama of American history)
Includes bibliographical references and index.
Summary: Discusses the economic, social, and religious reasons why immigrants, predominantly from northern Europe, and then from eastern and southern Europe, came to the Untied States. Considers incidents of prejudice experienced by these immigrants as well as contributions made by those of immigrant background.
ISBN 0 –7614 –0821 –5
1. United States—Emigration and immigration—History—Juvenile.
2. Immigrants—United States—History—Juvenile literature.
[1. United States —Emigration and immigration —History. 2. Immigrants—History.]
I. Collier, James Lincoln, date II. Title. III. Series: Collier, Christopher, date Drama of American history.
JV6450.C65 1999–
304.873'099'034 —dc21

98-3358
CIP
AC

Printed in Italy
3 5 6 4

CONTENTS

PREFACE

Over many years of both teaching and writing for students at all levels, from grammar school to graduate school, it has been borne in on us that many, if not most, American history textbooks suffer from trying to include everything of any moment in the history of the nation. Students become lost in a swamp of factual information, and as a consequence lose track of how those facts fit together and why they are significant and relevant to the world today.

In this series, our effort has been to strip the vast amount of available detail down to a central core. Our aim is to draw in bold strokes, providing enough information, but no more than is necessary, to bring out the basic themes of the American story, and what they mean to us now. We believe that it is surely more important for students to grasp the underlying concepts and ideas that emerge from the movement of history, than to memorize an array of facts and figures.

The difference between this series and many standard texts lies in what has been left out. We are convinced that students will better remember the important themes if they are not buried under a heap of names, dates, and places.

In this sense, our primary goal is what might be called citizenship education. We think it is critically important for America as a nation and Americans as individuals to understand the origins and workings of the public institutions that are central to American society. We have asked ourselves again and again what is most important for citizens of our democracy to know so they can most effectively make the system work for them and the nation. For this reason, we have focused on political and institutional history, leaving social and cultural history less well developed.

This series is divided into volumes that move chronologically through the American story. Each is built around a single topic, such as the Pilgrims, the Constitutional Convention, or immigration. Each volume has been written so that it can stand alone, for students who wish to research a given topic. As a consequence, in many cases material from previous volumes is repeated, usually in abbreviated form, to set the topic in its historical context. That is to say, students of the Constitutional Convention must be given some idea of relations with England, and why the Revolution was fought, even though the material was covered in detail in a previous volume. Readers should find that each volume tells an entire story that can be read with or without reference to other volumes.

Despite our belief that it is of the first importance to outline sharply basic concepts and generalizations, we have not neglected the great dramas of American history. The stories that will hold the attention of students are here, and we believe they will help the concepts they illustrate to stick in their minds. We think, for example, that knowing of Abraham Baldwin's brave and dramatic decision to vote with the small states at the Constitutional Convention will bring alive the Connecticut Compromise, out of which grew the American Senate.

Each of these volumes has been read by esteemed specialists in its particular topic; we have benefited from their comments.

CHAPTER I

A Nation of Immigrants

It is a truism to say that the United States is a nation of immigrants. The first English settlers, the ones who came in the 1600s, were, in a sense, immigrants. Just like millions of later immigrants, they had come to America to escape from autocratic governments, to find religious freedom, and to develop a more prosperous and satisfying life than they had had at home. It is true that some of the early arrivals, to Georgia, for instance, were petty criminals, beggars, and orphans sent by a British government who wanted to get rid of them. But the majority—not counting kidnapped Africans brought as slaves—were ordinary people who hoped to find in the New World comfortable livings, perhaps even riches, that they could not get in the British Isles.

So, through the 1600s and 1700s, immigrants from many countries came in a steady stream—a stream that shrunk and swelled as it went along, but never stopped running. Most of these first immigrants came from the British Isles—England, Wales, Scotland, and Ireland. An especially large number of Scotch-Irish came in the late 1700s. (The Scotch-Irish were not Celtic Irish, nor were they Catholic; they were Scotsmen

All Americans initially came to the New World from somewhere else. This reenactment, staged at the Jamestown Settlement in Virginia, shows English settlers in a military drill.

brought to Ireland by British overlords in the early seventeenth century.) But there were always people coming from other places, too. In 1790, when the first federal census was taken, there were 100,000 people with Dutch ancestors in the country, most of them in or around New York City, originally settled by the Dutch and a Dutch possession until 1664. There were over 75,000 Germans, the majority in Pennsylvania, with others scattered elsewhere. There were 14,000 French Huguenots, who had fled religious persecution at home, and pockets of many other nationalities everywhere. And beyond these voluntary immigrants were a very large number of involuntary ones—blacks imported as slaves from Africa and the Caribbean Islands.

America, thus, has always had its immigrants. But the great waves of immigration that began in about 1820, and went on for a hundred years, dwarfed anything that had gone before. It is these people we tend to think of when we use the word immigrant.

Historians have usually divided the great immigration of this period into two phases: the *old* immigration of about 1820 to 1880 (with the Civil War, which drastically slowed immigration, coming in the 1860s) and the new immigration of 1880 to 1920. Today we are seeing an even newer phase of immigration, from about 1970 to the present. It is probably better, then, to abandon the terms old and new and speak rather of first and second waves of immigration in the nineteenth century, with the current one called a third wave.

The first two waves differed mainly in the lands the immigrants came from. The first wave consisted of people from Ireland and Germany, but always with the largest number from England and Scotland, a majority of whom were Protestant. The second wave was dominated by Eastern and Southern Europeans, mostly Jews, Catholics, and Greek Orthodox from Russia, Poland, Greece, and Italy. Coming from different backgrounds, each group of immigrants has a different story.

The startling thing about all this immigration to the United States is not that it has brought with it problems—which it certainly has—but that is has worked as well as it has. No major nation in recent centuries has ever willingly accepted so large a number of strangers into its lands, especially strangers who in many cases have different folkways, customs, languages. Most people everywhere simply do not like having a lot of people among them who speak and behave differently from them. In the 1800s Japanese sometimes beheaded European sailors who were shipwrecked on their shores. The Chinese would not permit the ships of American traders they were doing business with to go anywhere in their country except to one or two special places on the seacoast. Even today no major nation permits anything like the amount of immigration allowed by the United States.

Why has America been so much more accepting of immigrants than other nations? At first it was because there was such a huge amount of empty land to be cultivated. (There were of course Indians living on this land, but because they did not farm most of it, the European settlers believed that it was going to waste.) Throughout the early nineteenth century, Americans felt that the country could grow prosperous only if that land was filled with farmers, hunters, and trappers who were growing wheat, corn, beef, and catching animals for their fur and skin. So immigration was unrestricted: Anyone could come who wanted, and those who came were allowed quickly to become citizens, vote, and hold office.

After about 1840, with the rise of the *industrial city*—the city we are familiar with today—reasons for admitting newcomers changed. Not all immigrants, as we shall see, went to the cities. But the majority of them did; the great waves of immigration of the 1800s are tightly intermeshed

The people pouring in from Europe and elsewhere saw scenes like this, and believed that America was filled with empty land, despite to the fact that the Indians were using it. This painting, by the celebrated artist Alfred Jacob Miller, who traveled through the West in the 1840s, shows a caravan at the Platte River.

with the old cities of the eastern seaboard as well as the new cities that dotted the frontier of forest and plains, especially after the Civil War. We need, thus, to know a little about how the cities that dominate American life today were born.

Very few colonial settlers came to build cities: Most came to farm, to hunt, to fish. But the prosperity of the American colonies depended a great deal on exporting the crops, livestock, fish, furs, hides, and forest products that the country produced in such abundance. Inevitably, small towns began to grow up around places with good natural harbors—Boston, New York, Philadelphia, Baltimore, Charleston. Merchants trading in tobacco, furs, wheat, and other products of field, forest, and ocean, built fine houses for themselves near the docks. To these little cities, too, came artisans and craftsmen, like tanners who turned skins into leather, and cobblers who fashioned leather into shoes. These craftsmen built workshops, often living in the second floor above their shops.

All of this activity attracted more specialized artisans and additional laborers—silversmiths, printers, cabinetmakers, and carpenters to build the shops and mansions of the rich, but also relatively unskilled teamsters to drive the wagons and carts from ships to warehouses and back, seamen to man the ships, and pick and shovel men, too. To the cities also came beggars and thieves who found the pickings there much richer than in small villages.

These early American cities were small. People traveled mainly by foot, and the houses of citydwellers had to be near the shops, warehouses, wharves. You could walk across these cities in a half an hour, or less.

At first these cities—towns we could consider them today—grew only slowly, though by 1790 there were over forty thousand people in Philadelphia—after London, the largest city in the English-speaking world; over thirty thousand in New York, and three other places had more than ten thousand. By the beginning of the Civil War, in 1860, New

Early cities were hardly more than what we today would call towns. Here is New York in the 1700s, seen in the distance. You could walk across the city, as it was then, in less than half an hour.

York, including Brooklyn, had about one million residents and Philadelphia over half a million, but only a few other cities exceeded one hundred thousand. But then, after the Civil War, there swept through American society a technological revolution the likes of which the world had never seen before or since. Led by the stationary steam engine, the railroad, the telegraph, the electric light, new systems for erecting tall buildings, the many-storied elevator, the electric motor, the telephone, and other inventions tumbling in one after another made possible the modern industrial city. (The industrial revolution is described in the volume of "The Drama of American History" called *The Rise of Industry*.)

On the basis of these inventions there was built in America a huge industrial system—great mills turning out products nobody had heard of a generation or two before—high-quality steel, sewing machines, electric dynamos, drill presses, and much, much more. This new industrial system was mainly built in cities—steel mills in Pittsburgh, meat-packing plants in Chicago, sewing machine factories in Bridgeport, Connecticut, cotton seed oil refineries in Memphis. For one thing, cities were crowded with the laborers needed to work in the mills. For another, cities were transportation centers where railroad lines met canals and ocean ports. In general, they brought together suppliers of a host of items that everybody needed from each other. It all worked together in one great system, and by 1890 or so the American industrial machine was the mightiest in the world.

This industrial machine needed workers. A lot of them came in from the farms around the cities, driven off by depleted soils in the East, low profit margins everywhere, and in a few places by new farm machinery that reduced the demand for labor. Tens of thousands of sons and daughters of farmers were drawn to the exploding cities by the glamour of the nightlife, nearby education and recreation, and a chance to have money of their own. But the demand for laborers was insatiable; it was obvious that immigrants from abroad could satisfy this need.

Moreover, it was understood that these immigrant laborers would work cheap. They were accustomed to hard conditions, so it was believed, and would be willing to accept low wages. What was not openly admitted, but was well understood, was that a steady stream of immigrants looking for work would keep wages low both for new arrivals and those who were already here.

In large measure, the great waves of immigration of the later 1800s were attracted by the new industrial city. The immigrants needed jobs, the factories needed workers. And so the doors were left open: Almost anybody (except the Chinese after 1882) could come to America who wanted to, and so they came by the millions. (In this book our focus is on voluntary immigrants. Africans, kidnapped and carried in chains to slavery, are the subject of the volume in "The Drama of American History" called *Slavery and the Coming of the Civil War*.)

CHAPTER II

The Irish Immigrants

One big question about immigration is this: Why did large numbers come to the United States from one country, and far fewer come from another? For example, why did relatively few people immigrate to the United States from Italy and Russia before 1880, and so many after? Why did the Scotch-Irish swarm in during the colonial period, but come in relatively meager numbers in the twentieth century?

The answer to these questions lies not so much in what was going on in the United States, but in conditions in "the old country," as many immigrants called it. (We should keep in mind that a person *emigrates from* his original place, and *immigrates* to his new home.) The first question, then, is not why did people come to America, but rather, why did they leave home? Ask yourself, after all, what would it take to get you today to leave the United States forever?

We can see the significance of local conditions very clearly with the Irish, the first of the massive wave of immigrants to reach America in the 1800s. Ireland was once, in ancient times, the center of learning in Europe. But its later history has been very unhappy. By the middle 1600s

England was firmly in control of Ireland. During this period many wealthy Englishmen were given rights to Irish lands by English rulers. These lands for ages had been farmed by Irish families, each on their own small piece, with their own cottage. Now, in addition to growing food for themselves, they had to pay rent to their English landlords. They solved the problem by growing grain, and raising pigs, sheep, and cattle for the market, which would bring in money to pay the rent with. They set aside a portion of their fields for potatoes, which provided a lot of nourishment for the amount of space it took to grow them. These Irish farmers lived basically on a diet of potatoes and some milk.

Worse off were the cottiers (cottage dwellers), who had no rights to any land at all, and had to rent small bits and pieces from year to year to grow enough food to feed their families. The cottiers were unbelievably poor. They lived in one-room cottages made of sticks and mud, owned hardly more than the clothes they stood up in, and lived almost entirely on potatoes. Often the fathers of such families would be forced to go to England to work during the harvests, while the mother and children wandered the countryside begging, and sleeping under hedges and in barns. By 1700, 80 percent of the Irish people lived like that.

Living in such conditions, the spirit of many Irish people was broken. They had no future; life for them seemed hopeless. Some turned to whiskey for solace. Others simply gave up, grew enough potatoes to keep themselves and their families alive, and otherwise did no more than they had to. From time to time these despairing Irish exploded in riots, which were usually savagely put down.

Unfortunately, the English rulers felt little sympathy for the mass of Irish living in poverty and degradation. Many believed that it was the best policy for England to keep the Irish poor. Nonetheless, they could not let the Irish starve to death by the thousands, so Parliament enacted "poor laws," to give the Irish at least minimum help. Because thousands upon thousands of Irish were in deepest poverty, the money needed for help was huge, and taxes kept rising. By the early years of the 1800s it was becoming clear to the English landlords that they would be better off to let the Irish emigrate away from the British Isles. Among other things, if the poor farmers were emptied off their land, it could be fenced in and used to pasture sheep and other livestock, more profitable to raise than wheat and requiring much less labor. Landlords began evicting their tenants, and at the same time the English government decided to help pay the passage to other lands for the evicted Irish farmers.

It did not seem that things could get worse for the Irish, but they did. In 1845 the first of a series of plagues hit the potato crop. There had been potato blights before, but the ones that came in 1845 and the years after were particularly devastating. Eighteen forty-six was an especially bad year, when almost the entire potato crop was destroyed, leaving "the land blackened as if the frown of God had moved across it." Disease swept through the hungry, weakened population. In these years well over a million Irish died of disease and hunger and another million fled. The population of Ireland was reduced by a third. (Think of ninety million Americans dying or fleeing today.) "In nineteenth-century rural Ireland," one historian reports, "the average age at death was only nineteen, and four-fifths of the population did not reach the age of forty."

Many Irish people, despite everything, loved their native land, as people generally do, and did not want to leave. But they had to chose between the real possibility of an early death at home or removal to somewhere else. So they began to come to America. The policy of the British government was to force emigrants to go to Canada, which was part of the British Empire. But there weren't nearly enough jobs there for the people swarming in. As it happened, many of the immigrant ships stopped at Boston. A lot of the Irish got off there and did not go on to Canada. Others who got to Canada turned around and walked into the United States. Soon the Irish were filling-up cities across New England. Others landed in New York and stayed there. Few of the Irish who

Right: This undated photograph shows a typical peasant cottage from County Antrim, Ireland. The woman at left is washing clothing in a bucket. Such cottages were heated by fireplaces, and had no running water or electricity.

Below: A contemporary engraving showing a mob of starving Irish people outside the gate of a workhouse during the famine times. The workhouses kept the inmates hard at work, but at least they were fed, while many on the outside went hungry.

reached the United States had much money when they arrived; many got off the ship with no money at all. As one historian wrote, "Like tired birds they landed here, bringing with them little more than memories of hunger and desolation and a flaming hatred of the English." Necessarily, they took the first jobs they could get, and stayed where they had landed.

Early immigrants of the 1600s and 1700s had come mainly in order to get hold of cheap land and set themselves up as farmers. Indeed, in the preindustrial era, as we have noted, the whole idea of open immigration had been to fill up the empty land stretching westward for thousands of miles. When the Irish first began flooding in around 1820, America was not yet industrialized, and there was still plenty of cheap land to be had. But the Irish did not take it up. For one thing, few of them had the money to buy even cheap land. But more important, they had suffered and starved as farmers, and wanted no part of it. Far better to take a job, any kind of job, that paid hard cash, than to be at the mercy of plagues and landlords.

As a consequence, the Irish immigrants mostly worked as laborers in unskilled jobs. Large numbers of them settled in cities, but tens of thousands of them dug by hand the famous Erie Canal across the unsettled plains of upstate New York in the 1820s, and other canals that followed. Thousands more helped to build the new railroad system spreading across the western plains.

But the Irish were also forced into low-paying jobs because many old-stock Americans believed that menial tasks were all that the Irish were suited for. And it is true that most of the Irish immigrants were illiterate, and had not learned in their rough cottage life the standards of dress and cleanliness that middle-class Americans were used to. Perhaps more important, the Irish were Catholics, and the great majority of Americans were Protestants. The antagonism that existed then between these two religious groups needs some explaining.

Up to around the 1500s, virtually all Europeans belonged to the

Some of the immigrant laborers lived in the most horrifying conditions, like this worker in a hovel under a dump. The photograph is by Jacob Riis, who did an important series of pictures of slum conditions.

Roman Catholic Church, headed by the Pope in Rome. But even before 1500 there were rumblings of dissatisfaction with the Catholic Church, for a variety of reasons, and through the 1500s groups began to split off to form Protestant sects. England, too, split from the Roman Catholic Church, for political reasons, and formed its own Anglican (or English Catholic) Church. Thereafter there was much hostility between England and the Roman Catholic Church. Indeed, at times England actually had to defend itself against attacks by nations still loyal to the pope. Although some Englishmen and women stuck with the Roman Catholic Church, most did not. Inevitably, most of the English felt a great deal of antagonism toward Roman Catholics.

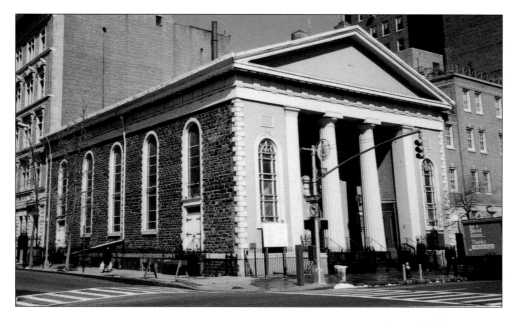

The Irish were responsible for establishing the Catholic Church as a major religion in American life. St. Joseph's Church in New York City was completed in 1833 in the Greek Revival style popular at the time. One of its priests, John McCloskey, became the first American to be named a cardinal.

They carried that feeling to the New World when they began to settle what would become the United States. (For the story of seventeenth-century religious strife in England see the volume called *Pilgrims and Puritans* in "The Drama of American History.") As a result, there was a lot of anti-Catholic feeling among the Protestants, who were the vast majority in the nation. And this, of course, worked against the Irish, too. "No Irish need apply," said signs everywhere, and searching for work the Irish immigrant often found "constantly that the fact that I was Irish and a Catholic was against me."

Yet despite everything, the Irish adapted to American ways. Unlike later immigrants, they spoke English (about half the people in Ireland spoke Gaelic, but many of those knew English as well.) Soon they learned to read and write it, and, like later immigrants, began step-by-step to make places for themselves in American society. But it was hard going at first.

A classic example of an Irishman who made his way upward was John Hughes. He was born in 1797 in County Tyrone, Ireland. His parents were farmers and linen weavers. When Hughes was a child, wars in Europe ruined the cloth trade, and the family was impoverished. In 1816 Hughes's father took one of his sons to America. They saved money, sent for John and then saved more and sent for John's mother and the rest of the family. John worked as a laborer, but managed to make friends with a well-known priest, who got him a job as a gardener at a seminary. A bright, ambitious boy, Hughes began to study Latin and in 1820, when he was twenty-three, was admitted to the seminary to study for the priesthood. In 1826 he was ordained.

At the time, antagonism toward Catholics was running strong. John Hughes began to write pamphlets, articles, and even a short novel defending the Catholic faith. He became well-known, and in 1838 he was named bishop of New York. This was a very prominent position. Hughes fought hard for the rights of the numerous Irish people in his area. He continued to debate and write, but his major interest was in education. He tried to get government money for Catholic schools, and when that failed, began to build the huge parochial school system that still educates tens of thousands of children in New York City. He also founded St. John's College, today famous for its basketball teams, and laid the cornerstone for St. Patrick's Cathedral on Fifth Avenue in New York, the most famous Catholic house of worship in the United States. In 1850 Hughes was made archbishop. His voice was now listened to in Washington. He corresponded with Abraham Lincoln during the Civil War, and was well-known in Europe, where he visited Napoleon III and his empress in the palace. When John Hughes died in 1864 he was one of the best-known religious figures in the United States. He had come a long way from weeding the flowerbeds at the seminary.

The story of John Hughes makes clear not only that immigrants could, and did, rise to positions of prominence in the United States but shows the growth of Catholicism into a major religion in the nation. Even though there was strong anti-Catholic feeling in the United States, there had always been pockets of Catholicism here and there. In particular, Maryland had been founded in the seventeenth century as a safe haven for Catholics being driven out of England and elsewhere. Nonetheless, the religion had been a minor one.

But as the Irish poured in they were followed by priests whose villages had been emptied out of parishioners by the potato blight and poverty. Like Hughes, other young Irish men and women turned to the church for their vocations. Bishops were appointed, parishes organized, and churches built. Over time Roman Catholicism became one of the strongest religions in the United States. And while other groups, like many Germans, Poles, and Italians also belonged to the Catholic Church in America, for a long time the Irish dominated the religion here.

Of course, few Irish immigrants rose to great prominence as Hughes did. Most had to struggle to find a foothold. But they had no choice. We must realize that many immigrants came to the United States with no idea of staying here. They came to earn some money, and go back home with their savings to buy a farm or perhaps start a business. Some 90 percent of Bulgarians returned to Bulgaria. So did large numbers of Italians. All told, during the 1820–1920 period, about a third of the Europeans who came to America went back to "the old country." Many even went back and forth several times as work and family obligations drew them home and sent them back. These "sojourners" were called "birds of passage."

But the Irish stayed. There was nothing for them to go back to—no industry, no land to farm. Many Irish missed their native land. They felt like exiles from their own country. Even today many people of Irish descent, whose families have been in the United States for generations, feel a sentimental attachment to the old country that is not felt by every immigrant group.

Initially most of the Irish immigrants were young, unmarried men who had no futures in Ireland, and came to build new lives for themselves. When the famines hit, the Irish began to come as whole families—a man would not leave his wife and children home to starve while he adventured in America. After the famines, particularly after the American Civil War, it was once again young people who emigrated from Ireland. Surprisingly, more than half of them were young women. This was unique among immigrant groups: Rarely in any group did more women than men immigrate to the United States.

But if there was little left in Ireland for men, there was less for women. They could not own land, there were no jobs for them; the only way many of them could live was to marry, and with so many men emigrating, it was not always easy to find a husband. In the years after the Civil War—a war in which thousands of Irish immigrants fought gallantly—there was greater acceptance of the Irish in America—especially in the servant class. In the United States there were plenty of jobs for single women, especially as maids and cooks in middle-class homes. One young woman wrote home, "My dear Father . . . Any man or woman are fools that would not venture and come to this plentiful country where no man or woman ever hungered or ever will . . ." (In the nineteenth century most middle-class families had servants.) Although salaries for housekeeping jobs were tiny, the girls would be fed and housed decently. They would, further, learn American manners and methods from the families they worked for. "Our Bridget" in the kitchen became a classic American figure of the time.

Whether it was Bridget in the kitchen, or Paddy digging canals or loading ships on the docks, the Irish Americanized themselves quickly. They had one great advantage over many other immigrant groups: They could speak English. This helped them greatly in politics. It has often been said that the Irish had a natural talent for politics. Not all historians agree, but it is certainly the case that as the Irish population in the big cities grew, ambitious Irishmen found a natural voting block to support them. By the post–Civil War period the Irish were becoming an important force in city politics, particularly in Boston, where Irish immigrants and their children were at times the majority, and in New York. By the twentieth century there were Irish mayors in many cities. The Irish were at home in America.

Two celebrated Irish politicians from Boston shake hands. At left, James Curley, Boston's longtime mayor. At right, John "Honey Fitz" Fitzgerald, politician and grandfather of President John Fitzgerald Kennedy.

CHAPTER III

The German and Other Immigrants of the First Wave

The second large group to come to America during the first great wave of immigration were Germans. Like the Irish, they came in a flood: Between 1830 and 1880 they were at least a quarter of all immigrants every year. They and the Irish, taken together, were the majority of immigrants during the first wave.

Deciding exactly who counted as Germans was not an easy task. Before 1871 there was, really, no German nation, but a collection of small princedoms and duchies populated by people who spoke German. But there were German speakers in other places, like Switzerland and Austria. Historians usually count as German immigrants those people who came from areas that were joined together as Germany in 1871.

Although, like the Irish, the Germans came in a wave, there were marked differences in much else about the two groups. For one thing, the Irish spoke English, the Germans didn't. For another, the Irish were almost all Catholics; the Germans were divided among Catholics, Protestants, and some Jews. For yet another, the Irish had long been acquainted with English ways—many Irishmen had spent time working in England. They were already familiar with the American culture that had grown out of the English one, and could adapt to it fairly easily. The Germans, in contrast, were proud of their old culture, which included the music of Bach and Mozart, and the writings of Goethe and Schiller. They did not want to give up their culture. As one historian has put it, German immigrants "came not to establish something new, but to reestablish something old." Finally, many of the Germans had owned farms or small businesses back home; they came with a little money and, perhaps more important, skills at crafts they could take up in America.

The German immigrants felt that they had come from a culture superior to the one they found in the United States, much of which was still wilderness land. They were proud of such heroes of art and literature as the composer Ludwig van Beethoven (left) and the writer Johann Wolfgang von Goethe.

But like the Irish, the Germans were impelled to leave their homelands by conditions there. By the early seventeenth century, much of the area along the Rhine River could no longer support its agricultural population, and then a series of wars seriously disrupted the economy and ruined the farms. Bad weather—especially in 1708 and 1709—heavy taxation and the fear of being drafted into the local armies drove thousands of Germans to emigrate. Another five thousand or so came to America as soldiers hired by George III to help put down the American rebellion in the 1770s and stayed on. Large numbers of impoverished farmers indentured themselves by signing contracts in which they agreed to labor for three to six years in America in return for the cost of their passage. They would work until they had "redeemed" their contract and thus were called "redemptioners." By the early nineteenth century, like most of Europe, the small German states were undergoing overwhelming changes due to the rise of industrialism. The railroads, and the new machinery and technology, were changing life drastically. As in the United States, new labor-saving agricultural techniques were taking away jobs on farms, pushing farm workers into city factories.

At the same time, for a number of complex reasons, population in the small German states was growing rapidly. Where in earlier times a farmer was often fortunate to have a son to carry on the farm after him, now he might have two or three sons to provide for. (It was assumed that daughters would marry some other farmer's sons.) If he divided his land among two sons, within a generation or two each plot of land would not be large enough to support a family. The only realistic choice was to leave the land to one of the sons, and hope that the others could find work elsewhere. As in America, many migrated to the cities to work in shops and factories. These people, already on the move, would frequently decide to emigrate elsewhere if they were not satisfied with the jobs they could find in German cities. Others, decided to go directly to another country. Germans were emigrating to South America, Russia, Canada, and some other places, but the bulk of them came to the United States, where, they were told, there were jobs enough for everybody.

Then, in the years after the American Civil War ended in 1865, new methods of agriculture and cheap railroad and steamship transportation dramatically reduced the price of grain from India, Russia, and the United States. Soon Europeans were importing a lot of their grain, which made life even more difficult for German farmers.

Finally, in 1866, one of the German states, Prussia, managed to get control of the other ones. The Prussians were warlike in their outlook, and began drafting a lot of young German men into the army. Many of them chose to emigrate rather than fight in wars that meant nothing to them.

There were other, less significant reasons for Germans to emigrate. For one, in 1848 a series of revolutions swept Europe. These were ruthlessly put down, and many of the leaders fled their homelands. A number of German intellectuals and politicians who had been leaders in these 1848 revolutions came to the United States. Again, some small religious groups came to America to found new societies for themselves, among them Jews attracted by Reform Judaism in the United States. But in the main, Germans chose to come to the United States in order to have a better chance of a good life than they believed they had at home.

We have said that immigrants tended strongly to settle in cities, to become part of the rapidly growing industrial machine. The Germans were an exception. Like the Irish, most of them were farmers, even though some had moved first from their farms to German cities. But unlike the Irish, and almost every other immigrant group, half of the German immigrants went on farming in the United States, especially in Ohio, Missouri, and Michigan. Furthermore, they tended to build, in their new country, little farm communities made up of people from the same area of Germany, sometimes even the same village. In Germany, according to the rule there, people from one locality followed the same

In 1848 Europe was swept by a series of revolutions led by intellectuals and students against the aristocratic rulers of numerous European nations. Many Germans were active in these revolts, and when the revolutions failed, were forced to flee their homelands. As a consequence, a considerable number of German philosophers and artists emigrated to the United States. The German immigrants had many more newspapers, and engaged in more cultural activities, than did most other immigrant groups. In this picture revolutionaries in Berlin are building a barricade in preparation for an attack by forces loyal to the king, Frederick William IV.

religion. The result was that in the United States areas where Germans built clusters of farm communities they were likely to be all Lutheran, or all Catholic.

Inevitably, these German communities tried to keep up their old ways, as well as their old religion and language. In some such communities German was the basis language for several generations, used in the schools, the churches, the homes. In some states these German farmers

While most immigrants from Europe settled in American cities, especially the cities of the Northeast, like Boston, New York, and Philadelphia, many Germans went to the Midwest and took up farming. This picture shows a typical farm of the day, with oxen pulling a wagon loaded with barrels of apples.

and their descendants dominated wide areas; they made-up over a quarter of all the farmers in Wisconsin, for instance. In time, of course, the Germans adopted American ways, and the English language. Nonetheless, the German communities have been amazingly long lasting. Over a third of the farmers in the United States today claim some German ancestry, and even as late as 1980 a quarter of the rural farm population in the Midwest claimed to be of *pure* German ancestry, an astonishing fact in a nation where people routinely marry "out"—that is, marry somebody from a different ethnic group from their own. Thus, we might think of these Germans—and some other groups, as well—who carried their culture with them and reestablished it in America as "transplanted" rather than "uprooted" as we might characterize other immigrants who had less choice about leaving their homelands.

The German immigrants who came to farm thus established self-contained communities that were very similar to the little farm village and towns they had come from in Germany. This by itself was an attraction for other immigrants, for people from, let us say, a little town in Bavaria or Saxony knew that they could find a village in the American Midwest where there would be the same religion, the same style of dress, the same sort of cooking, even the same dialect of German that they were leaving behind.

But of course half of the great flood of German immigrants who came to America in the nineteenth century, like most other immigrants, went to cities. Along with the Irish, many of them settled in New York City; but since many debarked at Baltimore and New Orleans, most of them landed in cities in the Midwest where there were fewer Irish, like Milwaukee, Chicago, Cleveland, and Detroit. Milwaukee, Cincinnati, and St. Louis were sometimes said to form a German triangle.

Once again unlike the Irish, some of the German immigrants arrived with skills in trades or crafts. Germany had long been noted for its beer, and brewing was one of the skills that migrated to the United States. Along with beer went the institution of the "beer garden," a place where Germans would gather, especially on Sundays, to eat, drink, and talk. One scholarly German complained that "wherever three Germans congregated in the United States, one opened a saloon so that the other two might have a place to argue." Many Germans set themselves up in the business of brewing beer, first for the use of their fellow Germans, and then for Americans as a whole. Even today, many of the best known brands of beer have German names.

Germans were skilled at many other trades, working as bakers, cabinetmakers, cigar makers, machinists, printers, artists, and musicians. More than a third of German-born workers practiced some sort of trade

New York was a primary entry point for immigrants. Ellis Island, established by the Federal government as an immigration center, is today a national museum. But in fact Ellis Island did not open until 1892. Previously, most New York immigrants landed at Castle Garden in the Battery, as shown in this picture. Originally a fort, Castle Garden was restored in the 1970s and is, like Ellis Island, a national monument, known as Castle Clinton.

or craft. Women, too, worked at certain trades, as laundresses, nurses, bakers, or as domestic servants in middle-class homes. But the majority of the German immigrant women, unlike large numbers of other working-class immigrant women, married and stayed home to care for their houses and their children.

The Germans who came to the cities, like immigrants of most groups, tended to form their own "Little Germanies" where they congregated. Such German city "enclaves" could not be as self-contained as could the farming communities: As was the case with "Little Italies" and "Chinatowns," there was always some mixture of other groups. Nonetheless, even in the big cities, the Germans fought to hang onto their language, culture, and folkways.

However, the German immigrants were by no means completely unified. They tended to form separate communities based on their religions. Indeed, there was often squabbling within these religious groups. Some much earlier German groups began using English in their Lutheran churches; the more recently arriving Germans strongly objected to this, and the Lutherans were split by the quarrel.

Most immigrants came to the United States crowded below decks in "steerage." In the earlier periods, particularly, the trip was uncomfortable and there was often sickness, even death, on board. But in the later days, as steamships took over from sail, the trip from Europe became swifter and more comfortable, although hardly luxurious. Here, passengers on the S.S. Patricia *dance on the decks in 1902.*

But despite the divisions along religious lines, the German immigrants managed to develop a surprisingly unified culture in their new homeland. By the 1880s there were about eight hundred German-language newspapers in the United States, a far greater number than any other immigrant group produced. German writers turned out a great many books—novels, histories, collections of short stories for German readers. There was even a large encyclopedia filled with information about German-Americans. The earliest newspaper comics were drawn by German cartoonists.

Germans had a particularly strong musical culture, going back to Johann Sebastian Bach, and even earlier. There were thousands of German musical societies in the United States, which put on songfests, chorales, even operas. In Brooklyn alone by 1900 there were almost two hundred singing societies. Germans, too, helped to develop many of the symphony orchestras that exist in most larger American cities. After all, some of the greatest writers of symphonies, like Haydn and Beethoven, were German. In truth, the Germans sometimes could be arrogant in their belief that German culture was superior to the culture of the land they had come into.

The strength of German culture in America was built on the large number of German intellectuals and writers who immigrated, many of them after the collapse of the European revolutionary movement of 1848. One such intellectual was Carl Schurz, one of the most famous German immigrants of the time. Schurz was not a peasant farmer, but came from an educated family, which sent him to a university in 1847. When the revolutionary movement began in 1848—when he was nineteen—Schurz joined it. He quickly became a student leader, and gave many speeches to his fellows. He eventually fought in the revolutionary forces. When the revolution was crushed, he managed to escape from the town he had been defending by crawling through a sewer, and made his way to Switzerland.

Then he discovered that a beloved teacher of his, who had also been part of the revolution, had been sentenced to life in prison in Berlin, Germany. Using a false passport, Schurz went back to Berlin. After many months in hiding, he was able to bribe one of the prison guards, and in the dead of night his old teacher was lowered from a high window to the street. He and Schurz escaped to England.

But it seemed clear to Schurz that the best hope for democratic government lay in the United States, and in 1852 he came to America. Very quickly he learned to speak flawless English. He plunged into politics, and began campaigning for office in Wisconsin, where there were a lot of German voters, giving speeches in both German and English. In 1858, through politics he met Abraham Lincoln, who was running for the Senate. Schurz was strongly against slavery, and two years later gave many speeches in favor of Lincoln, who was by then running for president. The Civil War broke out very soon after Lincoln took office. He made Schurz ambassador to Spain, where he worked hard to keep the Spanish government from supporting the South. Soon he was back home, where he was appointed a general and sent out to fight. He was personally brave, and led troops in some of the most famous battles of the Civil War, including the second battle of Bull Run and the Battle of Gettysburg.

After the war Schurz divided his time between politics and journalism, becoming a senator from Missouri and eventually secretary of the interior. In this position he established a policy of protection for the environment, and helped to start the great American national park system. At his death in 1906 he was certainly the best-known German immigrant to the United States, a man of honor and patriotism who had done a great deal for his adopted land. It was not until 1952, however, that an American of German ancestry was elected president: General Dwight D. Eisenhower, who ironically, became famous by leading the victory over Germany in World War II.

But of course most German immigrants were, like most immigrants from everywhere, plain people who struggled to get along. Today, millions of Americans can claim descent from immigrants from Germany who came to America in the nineteenth century.

A third ethnic group to come to the United States in large numbers in this first great wave of immigrants were the Scandinavians, over two million of them, about half Swedish, the rest Norwegians, Danes, and some Finns. Once again it was a story of exploding populations creating shortages of good farmland. From 1750 to 1850 the population of Sweden doubled, and it went up another 50 percent in the next half century. By 1870 almost half the rural population of Sweden owned no land, but had to work on other men's farms for small wages, or go without work at all. The situation was similar in Norway and Denmark.

Like the Germans, the Scandinavians headed for the Great Lakes and Great Plains areas of the Midwest, especially Minnesota, where even today there is a strong Scandinavian flavor. Among other factors, railroad companies encouraged Scandinavians to buy the land the railroads owned along their lines. Nonetheless, a considerable number of Scandinavians settled in cities, where they worked mainly as laborers. One city-dwelling Dane later to become famous as a photojournalist, Jacob Riis, described his arrival with little else but "a pair of strong hands, and stubbornness to do for two . . . also a strong belief that in a free country, free from the dominion of custom, of caste, as well as of men, things would somehow come out right in the end." The Norwegians had a strong seagoing tradition going back hundreds of years: Many of them worked as merchant seamen. And many prospered. "Norway," wrote one, "cannot be compared to America any more than a desert can be compared to a garden in full bloom."

One more group that came to the United States in large numbers before the Civil War arrived, not from Europe or Asia, but from the north—the French-Canadian province of Quebec. Canada had, of

Germans, Irish, and English shared many customs. These baked Christmas tree decorations are from Germany, and are similar to ones used in America at the same time. Because of such similar customs, it was thought that German, Irish, and Scandinavian immigrants would adapt more easily to American ways than immigrants from other countries who came to the United States.

course, once belonged to the French. With the British victory in the French and Indian War in 1763, Canada became an English colony, and English people began to fill up its land. However, there remained thousands of French-speaking people in Canada, mostly clustered around Quebec, some of whose families had been there for generations. To this day there has been much hostility between the French-speaking majority, to the point where the province of Quebec has repeatedly threatened to secede and become an independent nation.

However, it was not hostility to the English that led the French-

Canadians to emigrate, but poor farming conditions. The French-Canadians clung to old-fashioned farming methods that depleted the soil. Furthermore, as the population increased, small farms were divided among several sons into even smaller farms, to the point where they could not support a family. In the prosperous United States, south of the Canadian border, there were lumber camps, quarries, brickyards, all clamoring for workers. By the 1840s the *Quebecois* were flowing south, especially into New England, just across the border from Quebec province and less than seventy-five miles from the capital city of Quebec. It was easier for many French-Canadians to reach many American cities like Boston, about 350 miles away, than to get to other parts of Canada.

The Civil War gave French-Canadian immigration another boost. The North was offering bounties to recruits, and some 40,000 French-Canadians joined the union army, many of them already residents of the United States. The war, too, quickened production in the North, especially in the textile mills of New England, increasing the demand for workers. Recruiters from the factories went north across the border, sometimes hiring everybody from small villages, leaving them deserted. Beyond this, by the time of the Civil War there were good railroad connections between the United States and Canada. French-Canadians working in the United States would go home frequently to visit friends and family, impressing them with their new clothes, their gold watches, and such, that they had bought with earnings in the American mills.

As was the case with all immigrants, the French-Canadians brought something of their own culture to the United States: Living so close to Quebec, they could easily renew their contact with their culture often. For one thing, they had large families, and they expected their children from young ages to go to work. Children everywhere had always worked on farms, tending chickens, weeding gardens, picking berries, husking corn, so that the idea of children as young as six and seven doing some work was not unusual in farms all around the world. And indeed, there had been from the beginning of industrialization a considerable amount of child labor in the mills, especially the textile mills.

But native Americans had a long tradition of literacy, and made an effort to see that children got some schooling. The French-Canadians were more willing to put their children to work, rather than send them to school. The French-Canadians also had a tradition of being very supportive of their Catholic religion. They would contribute generously from their earnings to build new churches in the towns and cities where they congregated.

But like the Irish, the French-Canadians lacked education when they arrived, were often superstitious about having their children vaccinated, and were in general suspicious of government efforts to create healthy conditions for their families. As a consequence child mortality was higher among the French-Canadians than it was in other groups.

Nonetheless, despite the problems, the French-Canadians slowly became Americanized and prospered, although many continued to speak French among themselves.

The French-Canadians, however, were in numbers only a small portion of those of the first wave of immigrants who arrived in the United States before the beginning of the Civil War in 1861. Germans and Irish dominated, and these two groups would continue to come in large numbers all through the great period of immigration up to World War I. But by 1870 they would be feeling competition from other groups who were beginning to arrive in large numbers.

CHAPTER IV

The Second Wave Begins

During the years of the second great wave of immigration, from about 1880 to when immigration slowed drastically around the time of World War I, most Americans believed that there were very real differences between the people in these two waves. The first wave, dominated by Irish and Germans, was perceived as much like the descendants of the English who already occupied the United States. The Irish spoke English, knew English ways and ideas. The Germans spoke a language closely related to English, shared many customs, like the Christmas tree, certain Christmas carols, and fairy tales. They farmed in similar ways, ate the same kinds of meals. German composers like Handel and Mendelssohn were very popular in England and had even lived there. And, remarkable as it may seem, the English kings George I and George II, who reigned from 1714 to 1760, were Germans who didn't even speak English. Indeed, the English descended in part from German tribes who had come to England some fifteen hundred years earlier and had driven out the Celtic people living there. All these groups, as well as the Scandinavians, came from the northwestern corner of Europe.

By contrast, the immigrants of the second wave came mainly from Southern and Eastern Europe. This wave, beginning about 1880, was dominated by Russian and Polish Jews, Polish and Italian Catholics, and some Greek Orthodox. They spoke languages less closely related to English, and did not share as many folkways with Americans. Their styles of dress were different, so were their diets. The Jews seemed particularly foreign. They were not Christians, did not use the same alphabet as other Europeans, worshipped on Saturday rather than Sunday. There was a lot of feeling that such people would have a harder time adapting to American ways.

Today historians believe that these two waves of immigrants were basically not as different as was thought then. Nonetheless, each immigrant group had its own story to tell. While we look at the two main

Many of the second wave of immigrants dressed somewhat differently from old stock Americans, had different folkways, and different types of cooking. They appeared "outlandish" to Americans, who thought that these new immigrants would have more trouble adapting to American ways than earlier ones had. In this picture Polish Jews await passage to the United States.

groups from this second wave—the Jews and Italians—we must keep in mind that there were also coming to the United States people from dozens of ethnic groups worldwide—Poles, Japanese, Armenians, Filipinos, Hungarians, Chinese, and many more. In addition, Irish and Germans continued to come to the United States right along, although not in such large numbers as they had come before the Civil War. Indeed, up until the 1890s, German and Irish immigrants outnumbered the Italians and the Jews. As always, immigrants from the British Isles continued to make up a significant portion of the total.

The people of the second wave came to the United States for much the same reasons that had driven the earlier immigrants here: bad conditions at home. All of Europe was affected by a huge boom in population during the nineteenth century. In 1750 there were an estimated 140 million Europeans. By 1850 there were an estimated 260 million and by 1915 there were 400 million, despite the fact that tens of millions of them had left Europe to live in many places elsewhere in the world.

This population explosion was by itself a big problem, but as we have seen in the case of the Germans and Irish, changes in agriculture were making life increasingly hard for peasant farmers. Cheaper grain from the United States, Canada, Russia, and India hurt farmers everywhere. A rapid increase in Florida and California oranges and lemons cut into the market for Italian citrus fruit. French taxes on imported currants hurt Greek currant farmers, and French taxes on foreign wines were hard on Italian wine producers. Everywhere in Europe agricultural systems were changing, and farmers were suffering.

The plight of the Italian peasants, especially the farmers in the middle and southern part of the Italian boot, was not as bad as that of the Irish, but it was bad enough. For centuries much of the land in these areas had been controlled by large landlords, among them officials of the Catholic Church. For the peasants, the world beyond their villages hardly existed. Life was a daily round of long hours of toil in the fields hoeing, harvesting, taking care of cows, sheep, chickens, and pigs. They lived in small stone houses, in some cases not much more than huts with a single room. Food was cooked over fireplaces and water drawn from a well in the middle of the village. The young people grew up to marry the men and women they had known as boys and girls, and went on living as their parents and grandparents had lived before them. Always life was a struggle to scratch together a little money for a new piece of clothing, a holiday treat. There was no way for most such peasants to improve themselves, no escape, no way out—except to emigrate. One man recalled the hard life on his father's farm many years after he left Italy and came to Connecticut to work in a factory: "We start to work on the farm from 3:00 in the morning, milk the cow, to plough, and then work until sundown. That's why I left and come to this country . . . . Because I don't

As late as the 1920s, when this picture was taken, peasants in Italy were still tilling the soil using primitive wooden plows at the cost of much sweat, as their forefathers had done for generations.

like to work on the farm. It was too hard over there . . . it was too much, too many hours, for nothing. You worked for 10¢, 15¢ a day. I worked 20 hours a day . . . . "

Unfortunately, during the years of the early waves of immigration to America, various Italian laws forbade emigration. Then, late in the 1800s, these laws were, for complex reasons, liberalized, and suddenly there was an explosion of Italian immigrants coming to America. In 1880, 12,000 Italians had come; in 1907, 286,000 came. Between 1880 and 1913, more than 4.1 million Italians entered the United States.

Many Italian families came to America after spending generations without traveling much beyond the sound of the church bell in the village church. Others—perhaps most—came from cities, large and small. But none had ever seen anything like the great metropolises of the eastern seaboard of the United States. Such "vertical" cities of skyscrapers, elevators, and tenement houses did not exist in Italy.

This was especially true of New York, where by the 1890s the majority of immigrants first landed. Some of them have described their feelings when they first saw New York City. One Rumanian immigrant said: "I was bewildered at the sight of trains running overhead, under my very feet, trolleys clanging, thousands upon thousands of taxis tearing around corners, and millions of people rushing and pushing through the screaming noise day in and day out. To me this city appeared as a tremendous overstuffed roar, where people just burst with a desire to live."

A Lithuanian immigrant reported: "When I first arrived in New York the thing that troubled me most was whether I would be able to live in that heavy smokey air. [Coal was burned for heat and cooking and to drive steam engines.] It felt thick when I breathed it. When I looked at the people I thought that if they can stand it, I can. The things I looked at most was the big buildings and the busy look that everybody had . . . . Eating in a restaurant was something new to me and all the different kinds of food you could get was a great surprise. Privately I thought my

To people used to small, sleepy country villages, a great city like the ones pushing skyward in the northeastern United States came as a shock. Trains rushed over their heads, trolleys clanged past them, buildings taller than any they had ever seen towered over them. Many an immigrant felt lonely and homesick at being thrust into this uproar.

brother was very wasteful when he left a slice of white bread on a plate after we finished eating. I put it in my pocket with three other slices from my own plate. My brother laughed and told me that people ate white bread every day in America."

These immigrants were young, single men, as, for the most part, were the first arrivals from most immigrant groups. The Italians were no exception. Probably the majority of them came with no intention of staying. The idea was to find jobs, save some money, and go home. And about half of them did. But in time those who remained began to send for their families, with the idea of staying in their new homeland.

We must realize that up until the 1860s there had been no Italian nation as such, but a collection of small principalities sharing a language and culture. The situation was much the same as it had been with the Germans. The Italians at first tended to think of themselves as coming from this or that village, or region, like Tuscany, Calabria, or the island of Sicily. There was a tendency for people from one area to cluster in the same neighborhoods of the same cities in the United States.

But for these Italian immigrants, the greatest loyalty was not to the Italian nation, or to their old village, but to their family. Italians were intensely devoted to their families. Their lives revolved around them. Fathers were seen as family chiefs whose word was law.

This deep devotion to family was admirable, but it had side effects that were not always helpful in America. Among other things, many Italian parents distrusted American schools. They felt that it was the father, not the teacher, who ought to be the final authority on things. Fathers resented having their opinions corrected by schoolteachers. It

Like most immigrant groups, the Italians tended to cluster in their own neighborhoods, although other people were always mixed in. Note the shop signs in Italian in this New York neighborhood.

was also clear to Italian parents that their children were picking up ideas in schools that conflicted with Italian traditions and folkways. The strong American belief in the right of each individual to carve out a life for him or herself contradicted the whole idea of following authority and old traditions.

Indeed, the whole idea of education was foreign to many Italians: There had been few schools in their villages back home, few of the peasants had received much, if any, schooling, and they did not see the need for it now. Thus in Providence, Rhode Island, only 10 percent of Italian children went to high school, compared with 40 percent of other children. But of course in the United States education was the key to finding a good job and a place in the society, and the reluctance of Italian parents to have their children spend many years in school held the second generation back, and trapped them in lowpaying, toilsome jobs.

The Mission School, in the Five Points neighborhood of New York, which is now gone. There were at least one hundred fifty children in this classroom. Learning was by memorization, and the children were expected to sit quietly in their seats for long stretches of time.

Surprisingly, the Italians were not wholehearted supporters of the Catholic Church. Back home peasant farmers, however pious and God-fearing they may have been, saw the church as one of the authorities grinding down on them. The church, it seemed to them, had allied itself with the aristocracy and great landowners that were exploiting them. Moreover, the Catholic Church had opposed efforts to unify the little Italian princedoms into a single Italy. A unified Italy, the peasants believed, would be more democratic, and they strongly favored it. These immigrants arrived in America with a bias against the Catholic Church, despite the fact that the pope had traditionally been Italian.

On top of everything, in America the Italians discovered that the Catholic Church was dominated by the Irish; and where the Irish were not in control, the Germans were. In many instances the local parish priest could not speak the Italians' language. It was hard for them to feel a bond with a priest they could not communicate with. It was a long time before the Italian immigrants would find fellow Italians in the pulpit and the confessional. In the meantime they celebrated their own "saint's days" that tried to replicate the "festas" they had known in Italy.

A key figure in many Italian communities was the padrone (a word that can mean "boss"), usually an earlier immigrant who could speak some English, and had contacts with employers. Padrones were useful in helping new immigrants find work and settle themselves in other ways, but the system was easily corrupted. Many padrones demanded kick-backs and bribes from the workers they found jobs for. In time, however, as the Italian community grew, new arrivals were able to get jobs through friends and relatives, and the padrone system dwindled.

The Italians were slower than some immigrant groups, like the Irish, to get involved in politics. This was certainly due in part to their relative lack of schooling; but it was also due to the fact that so many of the Italian immigrants did not intend to stay in the United States. Not all who planned to return to Italy actually did so, but a great many did.

Furthermore, many Italian men were "birds of passage" who came over in the spring to work in construction, often laying bricks for the new tenements going up to house immigrants, and then returning to Italy in the fall, when the weather got bad. To build a career in politics you have to stay put—stay in a neighborhood, a town, a city, where the voters come to know and respect you. Furthermore, a politician of any ethnic group needs a base of voters who understand politics and can be counted on to vote. With so many Italian immigrants coming and going, or just plain uninterested, it was hard for Italian politicians to build such a block of loyal voters. But of course, in time, Italian politicians made headway. Paradoxically, among the first successful ones were James March and Paul Kelly, who had taken Irish names to sound more American. March, whose real name was Antonio Maggio, became Republican Party leader of New York City's Lower East Side in 1894. The Democratic Party leader was Kelly, born Paolo Antonio Vaccarelli. The first really nation-

Italian men were particularly active in construction, working to haul cement and lay bricks for tenements like these in New York's Greenwich Village, which became an Italian enclave. Apartments in these buildings, which once rented for a few dollars a week, are today very high-priced cooperatives.

ally prominent Italian-American politician was Fiorello La Guardia, who was elected to Congress from New York in 1916, and went on to become one of the most popular mayors New York City has ever had.

La Guardia, however, was born in the United States. One of the best-known Italian immigrants was Mother Frances Xavier Cabrini. She was born in 1850 in Lombardy to a comfortably-off family. She showed a keen interest in religion from childhood, encouraged by her sister Rosa, a teacher. She got some education, and began to teach. In 1877 she founded her own religious organization, known as the Institute of the Missionary Sisters of the Sacred Heart, and started a number of orphanages and schools all over Italy.

In 1887 she vowed to go to China to start a convent there. However, the Pope was aware that many Italian immigrants to the United States were falling away from the church, in part because it was dominated by the Irish and Germans. In 1889 the Pope sent her to New York. Once again she began founding schools, convents, and orphanages. Physically frail, she was nonetheless indomitable, and ceaselessly badgered her superiors to help her in her work. Her reach spread all across the United States, then to Central and South America, and cities in Europe. In the United States she started a series of charitable hospitals. She became an American citizen in 1909 and died in 1917. In 1933 she was declared venerable, the first step toward sainthood, and was canonized in 1946, becoming America's first saint.

Mother Cabrini was unusual in that she came from a family that could afford to have her educated. This was not the case for most Italian immigrants. In the Italian principalities the laws were made by the local princes for their own benefit and bore down very hard on the peasant families. As one Italian historian has written, "The upper classes lorded over and exploited the peasants whom they regarded as less than human. Toward the upper classes, the contadini (peasants) nourished a hatred which was veiled by the traditional forms of deference. Survival depended on seeming to obey the law while in fact living as much as possible outside of it—within the family circle."

Many Italians carried this deep suspicion of government and law to America. Perhaps this is why, regrettably, Italian immigrants have often been associated in the public mind with organized crime. The most famous of these crime groups is the so-called Mafia, or *Cosa Nostra*, but there were similar earlier ones like the Black Hand, which supposedly left the sign of a hand after it had assassinated someone. The very popular book and movie series *The Godfather* has kept alive the idea of Italian crime families.

It is certainly true that there has existed on the Italian island of Sicily an organized crime group called the Mafia. It is also true that many of the famous gangsters of the 1920s and 1930s, like "Scarface" Al Capone, were Italian. But so were many of them Irish, German, Jewish, and Yankee. The Italian involvement in crime has been very much exaggerated by movies, television shows, and books. As one son of Italian immigrants remarked, why should twenty-three million of us be characterized by the lawlessness of a few thousand? "It is instructive of the whole process" of stereotyping, writes one historian, "that one of the first major talking pictures on the gangster theme, *Scarface* (1932), based vaguely on the life of Al Capone (1899–1947)—born in Brooklyn of Neapolitan parents—was remade in the 1980s with a Cuban rather than an Italian character as protagonist." (Ironically, a Jewish-American actor, Paul Muni played the Italian gangster, and an Italian-American actor, Al Pacino, played the Cuban).

In the mid-nineteenth century, it was the Irish who were stereotyped as criminals; in our own day it is likely to be blacks or Hispanics. In fact, of course, most Italians, like people everywhere, struggled to raise their families as best they could under hard conditions in the land where they had recently arrived.

CHAPTER V

The Second Wave: The Jews

The second-largest group to come to the United States in this late-nineteenth-century wave were the Jews. The Jews have a special history. At the time there did not exist a Jewish homeland, like Israel today. The Jews were scattered all over the world, but a very large percentage of them lived in Europe, usually in their own neighborhoods, or "ghettos," as the term for a Jewish enclave was then.

Unlike nearly all other Europeans, the Jews were not Christians, but followed the Old Testament religion that Christianity had grown out of. Because of this, and because they followed their own codes in dress, worshiped on Saturday instead of Sunday, and generally appeared different to people of whatever country they lived in, there was a lot of hostility toward them. It is true that at some times and places the Jews successfully integrated themselves into European societies. In Portugal, in the fifteenth century and before, the Jews played important roles in government and in business. Similarly, Jews in the nineteenth century and well into the twentieth century were well integrated into the society. Many of them thought of themselves as more German than Jewish. In England, Benjamin Disraeli, a Jew, became prime minister.

During medieval days, there were a number of massacres of Jews. This medieval picture shows Jews being burned in a pit. The incident is imaginary, but it suggests the dislike of Jews many Europeans of the time felt.

But at most times and places Jews were reviled. During the medieval period there had been occasional massacres of Jews in Europe, and for the most part they had been kept on the edges of society. Things had improved for them by the nineteenth century, but not everywhere. Conditions were particularly bad in the area known as the Jewish Pale, or just the Pale, a large strip of land in Eastern Europe running from the Black Sea in the south, to the Baltic in the north. This land had at times been ruled by Poland and Lithuania, but by the late 1800s it belonged to Russia. The majority of European Jews lived in the Pale.

The Russians were especially hard on the Jews. Jews were not allowed, generally speaking, to own land, or in most cases to live in cities. They were therefore forced to dwell in small villages, called shtetels, mainly in the Pale. Because they could not own land, they could not became farmers. Instead, many of them made their livings buying farm produce, like wheat, cattle, sheep, milk, and vegetables, which they would turn into bread, steaks, and wool. They would then sell this produce to people in the villages, towns, and cities nearby.

A shtetl street in the village of Pruzana, Poland, taken in 1900 by the famous photographer Roman Vishniak.

Jews thus were almost forced into becoming butchers, bakers, and dealers in hides. Many of them necessarily became peddlers, carrying goods for sale in packs on their backs from village to village, from house to house. Others became crafts-men and artisans, working in gold and silver, as tailors making suits, and cobblers making shoes.

Even more than most immigrants, religion played a big part in Jews' lives: There were daily rituals to be performed, special ways that food had to be cooked and served. Particularly admired among them were their scholars, by which was meant people who studied the Talmud, Jewish religious law and lore. This admiration for scholarship was spread through the whole Jewish community. Males especially were supposed to be able to read Jewish religious writings and to be able to interpret the law. Not every Jewish man could, but on the whole the Jews were much more literate than the Russians they lived among. According to one survey in 1897, 50 to 75 percent of Jews could read at least a little, compared with 20 to 40 percent of Russians. Jewish boys were encouraged to study hard. Among other things, a young scholar of promise was a desirable catch, and might be able to marry a woman from a well-to-do family.

Women were not so strongly encouraged to study, but many of them got enough education to be able to read and write. Basically, however, they were expected to tend to their homes and their families, and to help out with the family business as necessary. In fact, a woman who married a fine scholar might have to run the family business herself while her husband pored over his religious books.

But despite the fact that most of these Eastern European Jews living in the Russian Pale were craftsmen or small businessmen, they were very poor, as poor as the Russian farmers living on the land around them. It is hard to earn much money as a peddler or a shoemaker when your customers are poor themselves.

Worse than poverty was the hostility they felt around them and the insults that the Russians frequently heaped on them. They always lived in the fear that they would be attacked by their Russian neighbors; and they sometimes were. In addition, the young men might be drafted into the czar's army for long periods.

Anti-Jewish feeling in Russia came to a head in 1881 when Czar Alexander II was assassinated. The Jews were blamed, though the assassin was not Jewish and very few Jews were involved in the antigovernment terrorism. The incident triggered what are known as *pogroms*—that is, massive attacks on Jewish villages during which Jews could be beaten, even killed. For example, a pogrom in the city of Kishinev in 1903 killed 47 people and wounded 424. Houses were burned, shops pillaged. These pogroms were unofficial, led by gangs, but in fact the Russian government favored them and looked the other way when they occurred. Many times police actually were leaders in the pogroms. The pogroms continued sporadically until the czarist government was overthrown in 1917.

The Jews, thus, had plenty of reason to leave Russia, and eastern

This engraving shows Jews being driven from their homes in a village in Podolsk, Russia, at the time of the beginning of a wave of pogroms in 1882.

Europe in general. After 1881 they began to pour into the United States in an increasing flood. The first Jewish immigrants had been German Jews who had come in earlier as part of the general immigration of the Germans. These Jews had settled mainly in cities, and were finding their ways in their new homeland. The German Jews were not exactly pleased by the flood of newcomers from Eastern Europe. They believed that, because of their German backgrounds, they had a higher culture than the Jews from the shtetels—the villages of the Pale. They also feared that a large flood of rough newcomers would trigger a rise in anti-Semitism in America, which it did.

These Eastern European Jews came to the United States with their own folkways and beliefs, just as had the Italians, Irish, and Germans. For one thing, very few had any experience with farming, so they were less inclined than even the Irish to go west looking for farmland. They settled instead in cities, especially in the Northeast, particularly New York and Chicago. In New York they crowded into areas like the Lower East Side, establishing their own synagogues, their shops and stores, their *schules* where Jewish boys could study Jewish religious works in their spare time.

The Jews had even less reason than the Irish to go back to Europe. They could not return to the shtetels where they were in constant danger of attack: 95 percent of them stayed in America. And unlike most other immigrant groups, there never was a time when large numbers of single

A scene from Orchard Street in New York, a celebrated shopping area for Jewish immigrants, here doing last-minute shopping for the Feast of Passover. Pushcarts like these were everywhere in big-city immigrant neighborhoods.

young men came by themselves. The Jews almost always came as families, or at least portions of families, with the rest to come when money for passage had been saved.

It has always been said that the Jews prospered in the United States quicker than other immigrant groups, and it is true that today income in Jewish families is higher than in many other American ethnic groups. Historians offer two reasons for this. One is the fact that Jews had been craftsmen and small businessmen in the shtetels. They had a tradition of buying and selling, of working as butchers, bakers, tinsmiths, cobblers. In the United States, many of them were able to go into business on their own. A lot of them began as peddlers, carrying goods for sale in packs on their backs. Others shoved pushcarts through city streets, buying and selling old clothes, junk, bottles, used goods of any kind. With a little success they would rise from a pushcart to a horse-drawn wagon to a small shop, and if they were lucky and hardworking end up running a retail business in clothing, furniture, jewelry, hardware. Where 50 percent of workers from other ethnic groups did unskilled work, and another 25 percent skilled industrial labor, less than a quarter of Jews did such work. Almost a quarter had their own businesses, and another 20 percent were artisans such as cobblers, tailors and the like. One of these, for instance, was Levi Strauss, who designed blue denim work pants for men headed for the California goldfields in the 1850s. This Jewish immigrant, then, was the father of the most characteristic American article of clothing, Levi jeans.

Not every Jewish peddler prospered; many remained poor. But others built up their business a bit at a time, and became quite successful. And when that happened, they would almost certainly see to it that their sons were educated. This was the second reason why so many Jewish immigrants crawled up out of the ghettos, like the Lower East Side of New York. As we have seen, Jews honored the scholars among them, the men who spent their lives studying religious law and lore. By no means were all Jews, especially the Eastern European Jews, well educated. Many of them were simply illiterate. But respect for scholarship ran through their society. They brought that feeling with them to the United States. As a result, Jewish boys, especially, were encouraged to study hard, and were often permitted to stay in school a year or two longer than the children of other immigrants. It must be remembered that most immigrants, working long hours, for low pay, and often blessed—or burdened—with large families, needed every penny they could scrape together just to pay the rent, and buy food and clothing. Whatever they thought about education, it was often necessary for young people to go to work at early ages.

The rules about school attendance differed from state to state, but nowhere were they as strict as they are today. For example, in the late 1800s in some places boys and girls did not have to go to school after their tenth birthdays. In some areas there were no rules about going to school at all. In many cases, where there were rules, parents, feeling that the money was more important than education, simply broke the rules. Both the Italians and the French-Canadians took this position. Very few towns and cities employed truant officers to enforce even the minimal requirements.

The Jewish immigrants, too, needed money as much as other groups, but at the same time they valued education more than some did. So where it was possible, they kept their children, especially the boys, in school. Beyond that, if a Jewish father began to get ahead a little in business, he was likely to use any extra money he had to send a promising boy, or even a girl, to college.

All of this was made possible by the fact that by the late 1800s many American states were developing excellent public school systems that were open to everyone no matter how poor. Schools were free, as they had not been back in Europe, where often there were none at all. And in places like New York City, where about half the American Jews lived, there were state and city colleges that were very cheap, so that even poor boys from immigrant families could find ways to scrape up an education. City College of New York, the famous CCNY, became an education haven for New York's Jews.

One important route out of the ghetto for immigrants was through the entertainment industry. Just as the immigrants were coming in, there was rising in the United States a brand-new show business. In the 1880s and after, the heart of this new show business was vaudeville, or variety—theatrical shows featuring brief acts involving singers, dancers, comics, trained animals, acrobats, jugglers. By 1900 the phonograph record was coming into its own, and shortly afterward, the movies.

Many middle-class Americans felt that much of this entertainment was vulgar and low class, and at first they would have nothing to do with it. This left the way open to the immigrants, and they jumped in. Jews, Irish, and Germans in particular began to take over, not only becoming musicians, singers, actors, and dancers, but writing the songs and producing the shows and movies. Many of the greatest hit songs of the twentieth century were written by immigrants.

One of the most famous of these was Irving Berlin, author of such famous tunes as "White Christmas," and "God Bless America." Berlin was born in Russia of Jewish parents who immigrated to the United States and settled in New York when Irving was five. Unlike some other Jewish boys, he did not get much schooling. Instead, as a youth he worked as a street singer, and then as a signing waiter in a restaurant in Chinatown.

In 1907, when Berlin was nineteen, he wrote a tune called "Marie from Sunny Italy," which was published. A few years later his song, "Alexander's Ragtime Band," became a big hit. By 1918 Berlin was writing songs for Broadway shows. By 1921 he was part owner of his own Broadway theater, the Music Box, and was putting on his own shows, using his own songs. When talking films came in the late 1920s, Berlin began writing music for movies, and by the 1940s, between his Broadway hits, his movies, and his songs, he was probably the most famous of all American songwriters. "White Christmas" is thought to be the best-selling song of all time. Berlin never really learned to play the piano properly, and needed help harmonizing his own tunes. But he had a great musical gift and used it to rise from the bottom of the heap to fame and fortune.

The importance of immigrants to the development of American show business is suggested by these sheet music covers. At left, the cover for Irving Berlin's first big hit, "Alexander's Ragtime Band." At right, the jazz classic "Tin Roof Blues," written by musicians from Italian, French, German, and Jewish immigrant families.

In looking at the Irish, German, Italian, and Jewish immigrants, we must bear in mind that during this great period of immigration, people came to the United States from scores of places. There were, besides the Scandinavians and French-Canadians, large numbers from Poland, from the Balkans (Albania, Croatia, Serbia, parts of Greece and Turkey and other nations in southeast Europe), from Hungary and Czechoslovakia (now divided into the Czech Republic and Slovakia), from the Middle East and many other places. Particularly important in the American West was Chinese and Japanese immigration. The Chinese came first at the time of the great California gold rush of 1849, and then were encouraged to come in the 1860s by the railroad companies that were pushing lines across the Great Plains and the deserts of the Southwest, over the Rockies to California. The Chinese could be paid much lower wages than American workers would accept, and a great many came. Immigration of Chinese was largely stopped by state and U.S. legislation in 1882 by which date about 300,000 had arrived in the United States. But for the first time major restriction of immigration into the country had been put into place.

The Japanese were at first forbidden by Japanese law to emigrate, but by the end of the 1800s that was changing, and a considerable number of Japanese settled on the West Coast, particularly in and around San Francisco, where they worked at manual labor.

These groups, too, had their folkways, their own stories to tell. But there are certain things that can be said about most, if not all, immigrant groups. One is that despite the tendency for Germans and Scandinavians to take up farming, the bulk of the immigrants settled in cities, especially the cities of the Northeast. True, a lot of immigrants went to New Orleans, which was a major port city: Irish, Italian, and German immigrants were plentiful there. The Asian immigrants tended to go to the West Coast, and the Germans to the Midwest. But the largest number settled in places like New York, Boston, Cleveland, Detroit, Chicago, and Philadelphia.

PERCENT OF ALL IMMIGRANTS BY REGION OF ORIGIN

	1820–1860	1861–1900	1900–1920
Northwestern Europe	95	68	41
Southeastern Europe		22	44
Canada	3	7	6
Asia		2	4
Latin America			4

FOREIGN BORN, SELECTED COUNTRIES, 1860–1920*

	British Isles	Germany	Ireland	Italy	Poland	Canada
1860	587,775	1,276,075	1,611,304	11,677	7,298	249,970
1880	917,598	1,966,742	1,854,571	44,230	48,557	717,157
1900	1,167,623	2,663,418	1,615,459	484,027	383,407	1,179,922
1920	1,135,489	1,686,108	1,037,234	1,610,113	1,139,979	1,138,174

*The figures in this chart represent the number of people living in the United States in the year given who had been born in the listed country.

Another similarity is that immigrants generally formed their own communities wherever they went, city or country. Most of the urban communities were not exclusive to one group. In every Little Italy there were likely to be some Germans, Irish, Poles, Bulgarians, mixed in. Nonetheless, one group or another tended to dominate a particular area. The main shops would be Italian, Swedish, Polish, or whatever, the signs

IMMIGRATION TO THE UNITED STATES 1820–1924

1820–30	151,824	1861–70	2,314,824	1901–10	8,795,386
1831–40	599,125	1871–80	2,812,191	1911–20	5,735,811
1841–50	1,713,251	1881–90	5,246,613	1921–24	2,344,599
1851–60	2,598,214	1891–1900	3,687,564	Total	35,999,402

% OF TOTAL U.S. POPULATION FOREIGN BORN 1850–1920

1850	9.7	1880	13.3	1910	14.7
1860	13.2	1890	14.7	1920	13.2
1870	14.0	1900	13.6	1990	8.0

% OF FOREIGN BORN IN SELECTED CITIES

	1860	1910	Foreign Born and their Children 1910		1860	1910	Foreign Born and their Children 1910
St. Louis	60	18.3	58.3	Cincinnati	46	15.6	52
Chicago	50	35.7	77.5	Buffalo	46	30	70.4
San Francisco	50	31.4	68.3	Cleveland	45	35	74.8
Milwaukee	50	29.8	78.6	New Orleans	38	8.2	30.1
New York	48	40.4	78.6	Newark	37	31.8	69.9
Detroit	47	33.6	74	Boston	36	36	74.2

in the shop windows would be in that language, and the language would be heard in the streets. In 1920, for instance, 80 percent of the industrial city of New Britain, Connecticut, were foreign born, mostly Polish.

Daily newspapers in Polish were published there and you could live your entire day (outside of school) hearing nothing but Polish spoken. Inevitably, such ethnic enclaves came to be called Poliana, Germantown, Chinatown, and Little Russia.

A third commonality is that most of the immigrants were at first poor, sometimes desperately so. We remember that one important reason for America's open immigration policy, as it still is, is to provide cheap labor for American farms, mines, and factories. In the view of many Americans, especially the officers of large corporations, there was no point in admitting so many immigrants if they would not work for low wages. And of course they did: Once they got to the United States they had no choice—except to go back. Many of them could not, or would not, return to the even worse conditions they had endured at home.

And so they came, and by 1920, out of an American population of about 105 million, 36 million—over a third—were immigrants and their children born here. And inevitably the question was raised: Was that too many?

CHAPTER VI

The Anti-Immigration Movement

The United States may have had an official policy of welcoming nearly everybody who wanted to come to the country during the period we have been looking at, but that does not mean that all Americans liked the idea. Right from the beginning there were always some—at times a good many—who objected to large numbers of strangers coming among them. Even before the Revolution was fought, at a time when the United States as such did not exist, many of those of English stock disliked seeing a lot of Scotch-Irish and Germans arriving. In 1798, when the nation was just getting started, a law aimed especially at the Scotch-Irish made it harder for immigrants to become citizens. It was, however, soon repealed.

A stronger burst of antiforeign feeling arose in response to the great wave of immigration from about 1820 to 1880. As an example, more immigrants moved into the little state of Connecticut in the ten years between 1850 and 1860 than had come in its entire previous history since 1634. Feeling, inevitably, was particularly strong against the Catholics, Irish, and Germans. Around the middle of the 1800s there coalesced around anti-immigration opinion a new political organization, called the American Party, but known as the Know-Nothings, because its members were instructed to answer, "I don't know," when anyone asked about the party's secret lodges. The Know-Nothings wanted to keep Catholics and foreigners in general out of public office, and asked for a twenty-one-year residence before immigrants could become citizens, on the grounds that people born in America could not vote until they reached the age of twenty-one. During the 1840s the Know-Nothings and earlier anti-immigrant groups gained a lot of support, elected their people to many offices, and got laws restricting immigration passed in some states. These laws were struck down in 1849 by the Supreme Court, which held that only Congress could pass laws about immigration. The Know-Nothings soon broke up over the issue of slavery, and during the Civil War anti-immigration feeling died down, as tens of thousands of immigrants bled and died, mostly in the Union Army.

But with the second wave of immigration beginning about 1880, Americans again became fearful that the flood of newcomers would drown traditional American ideas in new ways of thinking and behaving. Through the last quarter of the 1800s and the early 1900s, a great variety of measures were introduced in Congress, and city and state legislatures, to limit immigration and curtail the political activities of immigrants already in the country. Efforts were made to keep Catholics out of office, for fear that Catholic officials would "take orders from the Pope."

Many Protestants also objected to having their tax money used to support Catholic parochial schools, because these schools taught Catholic doctrine, which Protestants disliked. Catholics responded that the "common" public schools were, in effect, teaching Protestant doctrine. Eventually, tax support of parochial schools was ended.

But the main thrust of anti-immigration legislation was to cut down on the numbers coming in, regardless of religion. In 1875 Congress passed a law excluding criminals and some others from admission. In

This picture, by the famous political cartoonist Thomas Nast, expresses the anti-Catholic feeling held by many Americans. Bishops, wearing miters with crocodile teeth, swarm ashore to attack American children, as a public school in the rear crumbles, a reference to the rising parochial school movement.

1882 this law was broadened to include people with mental disabilities. In 1885 "contract laborers" were forbidden entry. These were people who had been recruited to work in a specific factory, mine, or other job before they came over. Labor leaders objected that they would be used at strikebreakers, as many were. They also noted that such immigrant workers would keep wages down, which of course was one reason why they were recruited by employers in the first place. Later laws excluded people with various physical disabilities, such as blindness and infectious diseases.

As already noted, many anti-immigration laws were aimed specifically at the Chinese, and later, Japanese immigrants who were coming in large numbers to the West Coast. Chinese laborers would work for low wages in poor conditions. Many were hired to help build the railroads being pushed across the western plains, and a lot had stayed. They were especially disliked because their ways seemed even more "foreign" than anyone from Europe, and because, it was feared, they would take jobs away from American workers. In 1882 Congress passed the Chinese Exclusion Act, but loopholes in the law made it ineffective. There were

A large number of Chinese laborers were brought in to work on the railroads that were spreading across the Great Plains and over the mountains to the Pacific Ocean. These laborers would work for low wages, and there was much feeling against them by workingmen and their leaders, who felt that they would lower wages.

anti-Chinese riots and tighter laws were passed. There was a similar dramatic increase in Japanese immigration in the 1890s; more laws were passed to reduce Japanese immigration and to make it difficult for them to own land or become citizens. Many Americans thought that Asians would be hard to fit into American society and believed they should not be allowed to become citizens.

Longtime Americans did not easily welcome the newcomers into their midst. In the 1800s and into the 1900s, many Americans of English or German stock felt disgraced if a child married an Irish person. They considered the idea of marrying a Jew or Italian even more disgraceful. Nor did they always like the idea of having people from immigrant families living and working among them. Well into the twentieth century it remained difficult for Jews to buy houses in the more well-to-do communities. Similarly, it was, for some time, hard for people from Jewish, Italian, Polish, or other ethnic European backgrounds to get jobs in prestigious law firms, banks, as executives in large corporations, or gain membership in golf, tennis, figure skating, and other clubs.

It must be said that immigrant groups were equally as unaccepting of each other as the established Americans were. The Irish and Italians quarreled constantly over dominance in the Catholic Church. Many Catholics were anti-Jewish, insisting that the "Jews killed our Lord." Ethnic groups that were at odds in Europe, like the Greeks and the Turks, continued to quarrel in America. Indeed, it is almost a rule that two ethnic groups living in the same neighborhood will mistrust each other.

For many of the immigrants, the answer was not to look for jobs in established companies, but to start their own businesses. The well-known Bank of America was founded by an Italian immigrant, and was originally known as the Bank of Italy. Immigrants found a particular welcome, as we have seen, in the new entertainment business, which many old-stock Americans felt was undignified. Jews, Irish, and Germans played major roles in developing the popular song, the movies, and the variety show on which modern entertainment was based. By the 1930s they were making their way in professional sports. Names like Gehrig, DiMaggio, and Greenberg dominated big-league baseball in the 1930s and 1940s. But in the mainstream business world, immigrants often had to struggle for acceptance.

It must be understood that the anti-immigration attitude of many Americans was not unusual. Few people anywhere welcome newcomers readily. Most people resent having their neighborhoods, villages, and towns swarming with strangers with different ways, languages, manners of dress. Americans of long standing, who found the streets, shops, playgrounds of their childhood filled with foreigners, resented it. Indeed, immigrants who had established their own Germantowns or Little Italies disliked seeing newcomers from different ethnic groups move into what they had come to believe was their neighborhood.

Another major concern of old-stock Americans was that many of the immigrants did not understand American democracy. Italians, Chinese, Jews, and many others had come from places where governments ground down on them harshly. They saw *any* government as the enemy. They often did not understand that in America governments were supposed to be the servants of the people, and often actually were. Given some immigrants' attitude toward government, it is not surprising that when the rules of their own cultures came into conflict with American law, they ignored the law. They seemed, correctly or not, to many Americans to be lawless.

This anti-immigration feeling came to a head in the late 1890s, as the second wave of immigration was rising toward its peak in 1907, when 1,285,000 foreigners poured into America. Many Americans—probably a majority of nonimmigrants—insisted that the immigrants of this second wave, dominated by people from Southern and Eastern Europe, were inferior to the people of Northwestern Europe, like the English, Germans, Irish, and Scandinavians who had made up the bulk of the first wave. It was believed, as one person wrote, that the second-wave immigrants had a "higher percentage of inborn socially inadequate qualities than do older stocks."

In order to slow the flow of immigrants, people began proposing literacy tests for them. During the first years of the twentieth century a number of bills were passed by Congress requiring that immigrants be able to read and write in at least their own language. All such bills were vetoed by presidents, for a variety of reasons.

But the tide of immigration ran higher still. The cities of the Northeast were particularly affected. By 1890 New York City had twice as many Irish as Dublin, as many Germans as Hamburg, half as many Italians as Naples. In 1910 about three-fourths of the populations of Chicago, Detroit, Cleveland, and Boston were foreign born and their children. In 1916, 72 percent of the people in San Francisco spoke a foreign language. In 1860 nearly half (48 percent) of the people in New York City had been foreign born; in 1910, though the total population was six times as great, the portion of foreign born was still 40 percent. By 1890 nearly 15 percent of everyone living in the United States had been born abroad—a proportion that continued until the eve of World War I in Europe, 1913.

By then most Americans felt that this was too many. The tipping point came with the entry of America into World War I to fight against Germany. German-Americans, by this time well accepted by most old Yankees, found themselves reviled by other Americans of all sorts of backgrounds. German language courses, formerly very popular, were dropped from schools and colleges. German-American societies were banned, German newspapers stopped publishing. In 1917 a literacy bill finally became law, but it proved ineffective—only a tiny percentage of immigrants was kept out by it.

By 1920 nearly 35 percent of the American population was foreign born or their children—that is, first- or second-generation Americans.

This World War I poster for war bonds shows a helmeted German soldier taking a Belgian child prisoner. Rumors that German troops were butchering children in Belgium swept the United States, but turned out to be untrue.

REMEMBER ·BELGIUM·

Buy Bonds
Fourth
Liberty
Loan

Popular demand among much of the other 65 percent of the population for real curbs on immigration was irresistible. Among other things, many Americans believed that a lot of the immigrants were hotheaded radicals, socialists, anarchists. In truth, there were among the immigrants some radicals, but they were a tiny number. However, the press made a great issue of the bearded, bomb-throwing anarchists. Italians, in particular, were persecuted. Writes one historian, "Between 1891 and 1914 Italian-Americans were lynched in New Orleans, murdered in Colorado, beaten in Mississippi, and shot by mobs in Illinois." Both old-line Yankees and newer Irish and German Americans viewed the most recent arrivals from Southern and Eastern Europe as a threat to the "American way of life." In 1920 a strong law against immigration was passed. Then came the

American newspapers were full of cartoons of bearded, bomb-throwing immigrants determined to reduce the nation to anarchy. While there were a few anarchists among the immigrants, they were not more than a handful.

famous Immigration Act of 1924. This law set quotas for each country according to a formula that heavily favored immigrants from northwestern Europe against those from elsewhere. Quotas for places like England were much larger than the number there who wanted to come to America, while quotas for other places were smaller. The net effect was to reduce immigration to a trickle.

Actually, as many historians have pointed out, immigration was winding down anyway. World War I had cut into it drastically, and a financial depression immediately after the war, when jobs were in short supply, held it down. With the Great Depression of the 1930s immigration was reversed, with more foreign-born people leaving than arriving. Whatever the case, for forty years from 1924 to 1965, when more open immigration laws were passed, immigration was not nearly so significant a factor in American life as it had been during most of the nation's previous history.

It must be borne in mind that those opposed to immigration included a lot of people whose parents or grandparents had been immigrants—or indeed were immigrants themselves. Many of the first wave of German, Irish, and Scandinavian immigrants agreed that the later arrivals in the second wave from southern and eastern Europe were indeed inferior. Laboring people and their leaders saw that big business was using new immigrants to break strikes and keep wages down. The important labor leader Samuel Gompers was firmly for limiting immigration to protect workers already here, even though he had himself immigrated from England as a youngster.

The immigration policies of the United States have, from quite early, raised two difficult questions. One is how many immigrants should be allowed in, and who they should be. The second question involves *assimilation*, a word meaning to be absorbed into another body. How much should immigrants be expected to adopt American ways, ideas, the English language? How many of their old ways, old traditions, and their culture ought they hang onto?

To deal with the last question first, there have been two basic theories of assimilation. The "melting pot" theory says that everybody in the country, immigrants and old stock, ought to be blended together, so that everybody speaks English, follows the same—though changing—ideas, traditions and lifestyles. To some, the melting pot means that the immigrants should adopt the old American ways. To others, the melting pot means that a unified culture would be created by the blending of all cultures present in America, which would not be the same as the old American culture. But in either case, there would be a single culture for everybody.

The "mixing bowl" theory means that everybody would mingle, but that each person would hang onto his or her own culture, just as the lettuce, tomatoes, and cucumbers in a salad retain their own shapes, colors, and flavors while mingling in the same bowl. Needless to say, most first-generation immigrants have wanted to hang onto their own cultures, even their own languages, as much as they could. Most human beings, wherever they are raised, like to think that their own ways, ideas, and beliefs are the "right" ones. We are very reluctant to give up our cultures, our languages, even small customs like how we celebrate birthdays and greet each other when we meet on the street. Most immigrants fought off assimilating when they could. Some groups, like Catholics, Jews, and German Lutherans, established schools for their children to teach the old language, customs, and religion. Most immigrants continued to speak their old language at home, and many learned only enough English to get them through the day. Immigrants continued to celebrate the holidays of their homelands—the Chinese New Year, Jewish Passover, the Irish St. Patrick's Day. Most of them tried very hard to encourage their children to "marry in"—that is, marry one of their own.

But there was a strong push toward assimilation, too. Immigrants who wanted to rise in American society had to learn to speak and read English fairly well. They had to adopt American ways of doing business. For example, Jewish businessmen had a tradition of bargaining over prices, where in America there were fixed prices for most things. Immigrants who wanted to enter politics had to understand governmental machinery and American democracy, which were much different from the autocratic nations many of them had come from.

Of course immigrants could do fairly well for themselves without assimilating very much, by starting little businesses in their own ethnic neighborhoods, or working for one of their own people. But to advance very far, they had to assimilate to a considerable extent.

Many immigrants did not think it was worth it. Their loyalty to their traditional cultures was stronger than their ambition to rise in their new

Immigrants usually clustered in their own neighborhoods, and even today, the descendants of immigrants who arrived two or three generations earlier still inhabit such neighborhoods. Here, a scene from New York's Chinatown.

society. But their children, who usually went to public schools for at least a few years, were likely to assimilate more than their parents had, learning to speak English and studying American history and the democratic system, rather than the history of their parents' countries. Perhaps most of all, it was the desire for material goods that made Europeans into Americans. By the second generation, immigrants' children lived in apartments and houses furnished in ways unheard of in the rural villages of their parents' homelands. They played American sports, absorbed American entertainment, and yearned for larger houses and fancier automobiles. By the third generation, the pull of the old country was likely to be, for these grandchildren of immigrants, fairly small. While it is certainly true that some later generations looked back to the old cultures to find traditions and attitudes of value, nonetheless, by the third generation, the old country, whether it was Italy, Hungary, or Wales, did not seem to have much to do with them anymore, though they often continued to eat "ethnic" food, and keep alive at least the echo of their grandparents' culture.

We can see the effects of Americanization in the rates of "marrying out" of the ethnic group. A 1963 study showed that for six immigrant groups, half the grandchildren of immigrants were marrying somebody from a different ethnic group. For the Irish it was 75 percent. Among the Jews, in 1910 only 1 percent married outsiders; by 1970 it was almost a third and today it is over a half. At the end of the twentieth century most married Asians under the age of thirty-five had non-Asian spouses. Willy-nilly, even by the mid-twentieth century, the descendants of the immigrants were moving into the mainstream.

They were encouraged to do so by a number of institutions, both government and private, that were established as the tide of immigration was rising at the end of the 1800s. Among these were the settlement houses set up to teach immigrants American ways. The famous Hull House in Chicago, founded by Jane Addams in 1889, offered classes in English, bands for schoolchildren playing American marches and popular songs, classes in American cooking. Almost all states sponsored "Americanization" classes held at night in the urban public schools.

It is obvious, of course, that no society will work very well if a lot of people don't obey the law, a statement most immigrants would agree with. It also seems clear that American freedoms will be in trouble if people do not understand how a democracy works, and how it came to be. Historians agree that in America everybody ought to understand and live by the basic principles set down in the Declaration of Independence and the Constitution, with its Bill of Rights. Many people who have considered these things carefully go further. They believe that all Americans, newcomers or not, ought to live by certain "core" values embedded in

Most people agree that all Americans need to understand and support the basic ideas of democracy in order to preserve our form of government and the freedoms it guaranteed. Some of those ideas are set forth in the Declaration of Independence, shown above in this famous picture as it was being signed.

Many of the ideas in the Constitution were brought to the Constitutional Convention by James Madison (left). Basic to all of Madison's thinking was the idea of the Rule of Law, rather than the Rule of Men. That is to say, no person, like a king or president, can put forth an order unless it conforms to a constitution, or other laws passed in a democratic fashion.

these great documents, like the idea that the majority rules and we must follow the law whether we agree with it or not, or that everybody has a right to "life, liberty, and the pursuit of happiness," as the Declaration of Independence puts it. Certainly everybody ought to be able to understand English, even though they may choose to speak other languages at home, or with friends.

Many Americans believe that immigrants, however much they cling to their old ways in some respects, ought to accept certain basic ideas, like those embodied in the Declaration of Independence. Here, the signatures on that famous document.

Finally, it is always a question of how much diversity can exist in a given society. Most people agree that in a democracy there ought to be very great tolerance for different ideas, different ways of doing things. But on other questions there is less agreement. Does it make for greater happiness if everybody in the country thinks of themselves as Americans first, and only secondarily as Jewish, Irish, Polish, Italian, Chinese? How well can any society work when different groups of people are operating by different rules, speaking different languages? These questions are well worth debating.

When we look at the immigration of the 1820–1920 period, one thing we can see clearly is that in time the children, grandchildren, great-grand-children of those immigrants came to speak one language, and understand the rule of law embedded in our basic documents. It is getting ahead of the story, but we should see than in the decades after World War I, when immigration was cut to a trickle, all those people named Weinberg, Simonetti, Herbst, and Yablonski were welded into a unified nation.

This does not mean that all immigrants totally abandoned their old cultures. Irish-Americans, Italian-Americans, and many others continued to feel a kinship with "their own" people several generations after their forebears came to America. Many American Jews take great pride in the accomplishments of Israel, a nation that did not exist when their grand-parents and great-grandparents arrived. Perhaps the majority of Americans keep up some traditions and folkways from their pasts. Many Jews, even those who do not regularly attend temple, will light a meno-rah at Hanukkah; Italian-Americans still put on festivals to celebrate various saint's days; Chinese continue to eat traditional foods.

Yet, despite the continuation in all ethnic groups of certain old tradi-tions, the descendants of the immigrants of the great waves of 1820 to 1920 share a common American culture, sending their children to the same schools and colleges, wearing the same kind of clothing, spending their spare time watching the same television shows, working at the same kind of jobs in factories and offices.

But that shared culture is not the one their forebears found in America when they arrived, for many of their values, ways of thinking, and customs became part of the new American culture they helped to cre-ate, a culture that continues to change, generation by generation. The immigrants played the major role in creating the modern entertainment business. They brought to America dim sum, hot dogs, lasagna, bagels. They added such sports as figure skating, gymnastics, skiing. Over the decades after 1920 the children and grand-children of the immigrants were sitting in Congress, lecturing at universities, running large corporations. And in 1960 the great-grandchild of Irish-Catholic immigrants, John F. Kennedy, was elected president of the United States.

At left, President John F. Kennedy, with former President Dwight Eisenhower. Eisenhower was the first descendant of German immigrants to be elected president; Kennedy was the first Catholic president.

At any given moment there are millions of foreign born immigrants in America—twenty-five million at the turn of the century; it may seem that the United States is more of a mixing bowl than a melting pot. But we can be sure that the grandchildren of these newcomers will live lives and view the world much as do their friends whose families have lived in North America for three centuries or more.

BIBLIOGRAPHY

For Students

Anderson, Kelly C. *Immigration.* San Diego, Calif.: Lucent Books, 1993.

Brownstone, David M. *The Chinese-American Heritage.* New York: Facts on File, 1988.

———. *The Jewish-American Heritage.* New York: Facts on File, 1988.

Caroli, Betty Boyd. *Immigrants Who Returned Home.* New York: Chelsea House, 1990.

Cavan, Seamus. *The Irish-American Experience.* Brookfield, Conn.: Millbrook Press, 1993.

Fisher, Leonard Everett. *Ellis Island: Gateway to the New World.* New York: Holiday House, 1986.

Hoobler, Dorothy, and Thomas Hoobler. *The German American Family Album*. New York: Oxford University Press, 1996.

——. *The Irish American Family Album*. New York: Oxford University Press, 1995.

——. *The Italian American Family Album*. New York: Oxford University Press, 1994.

Jacobs, William Jay. *Ellis Island: New Hope in a New Land*. New York: Scribner, 1990.

Katz, William Loren. *The Great Migrations, 1880–1912*. Chatham, N.J.: Raintree Steck-Vaughn Pubs., 1992.

Lawlor, Veronica, ed. *I Was Dreaming to Come to America: Memories from the Ellis Island Oral History Project*. New York: Viking, 1995.

Meltzer, Milton, ed. *The Jewish Americans: A History in Their Own Words*. New York: Crowell, 1982.

O'Neill, Teresa, ed. *Immigration: Opposing Viewpoints*. San Diego, Calif.: Greenhaven Press, 1992.

Sandler, Martin. *Immigrants*. New York: Harper Collins, 1995.

Takai, Ronald T. *Journey to Gold Mountain: The Chinese in Nineteenth-Century America*. New York: Chelsea House, 1994.

Young, Carrie. *Nothing to Do But Stay: My Pioneer Mother*. New York: Doubleday, 1993.

For Teachers

Archdeacon, Thomas J. *Becoming American: An Ethnic History*. New York: Free Press, 1984.

Daniels, Roger. *Asian America: Chinese and Japanese in the United States since 1850*. Seattle: University of Washington Press, 1990.

————. *Coming to America: A History of Immigration and Ethnicity in American Life*. New York: Harper Collins, 1991.

Dinnerstein, Leonard and David M. Reimers. *Ethnic Americans: A History of Immigration and Assimilation*. New York: Harper and Row, 1975.

Higham, John. *Send These to Me: Immigrants in Urban America*. Rev. ed. Baltimore: Johns Hopkins, 1984.

Kraut, Alan M. The Huddled Masses: *The Immigrant in American Society 1880–1921*. Arlington Heights, Ill.: Harlan Davidson, 1982.

Miller, Kirby P. *Emigrants and Exiles: Ireland and the Irish Exodus to North America*. New York: Oxford University Press, 1988.

Payton, Shelia, et al. *Cultures of America. 15 vols.* Tarrytown, N.Y.: Marshall Cavendish, 1994–96.

Pitkin, Thomas M. *The Keepers of the Gate: A History of Ellis Island*. New York: New York University Press, 1975.

Smead, Howard. The Peoples of North America. 24 vols. New York: Chelsea House, 1986-91.

Stave, Bruce M., and John Sutherland. *From the Old Country: An Oral History of European Migration to America*. New York: Twayne Publishers, 1994.

Thernstrom, Stephan. *Harvard Encyclopedia of American Ethnic Groups*. Cambridge, Mass.: Harvard University, 1980.

INDEX

"poor laws," 17–18
potato crop, 18
presidents, 69, 84, **84**
prices, 78
Protestants
 Anglican, 21–22
 and Catholics, 68–69, 72
 German, 27, 31
Providence, Rhode Island, 49
Prussia, 30

Quebec, 38–40
quotas, 76

radicals, 75
railroads, 20, 30, 40, 64, **71**
religion, 11, 20–22. *See also* Catholics;
 Greek Orthodox; Jews; Protestants
religious persecution, 10
revolutions, European, 30, **31**, 36
Riis, Jacob, **21**, 38
Russia, 55, 57, **58**
Russians, 11

Sacred Heart, Missionary Sisters of the, 52
St. John's College, 23
St. Joseph's Church, **22**
St. Louis, Missouri, 33
St. Patrick's Cathedral, 23
salaries, 25
saloons, 33
Scandinavians, 38, **39**
Scarface, 53
schools. *See also* education
 attendance, 61
 German, 31, 78
 in New York City, 23, **49**, 59
 parochial, 23, 69, **70**, 78
 public, 61–64, 79
schules, 59
Schurz, Carl, 36–37
Scotch-Irish, 9–10, 68
Scottish, 9, 11
seamen, 38
Serbs, 64
servants, 25
ships, **35**
show business, 62–63, **63**
slaves, 10
slums, **21**

small business, 60, 72, 78
socialists, 75
"sojourners," 24, 47, 50
sports, 73, 79, 83
steamships, **35**
stereotypes, 53
Strauss, Levi, 60
Supreme Court, 69
Swedes, 38

technology, 14
textile mills, 40
"Tin Roof Blues," **63**
towns, 13
traders, 13
tradesmen, 33–34, 51, **51**
travel conditions, **35**
Turks, 64

Vaccarelli, Paolo Antonio, 51
vaccinations, 41
values, 80–81
vaudeville, 62
violence, 75
voting, 69

wages, 15, 64, 67, 70, 77
Wales, 9
West Coast, 64, 71
"White Christmas," 62–63
wine, 44
women
 German, 34
 Irish, 25
 Jewish, 57
workers. *See also* artisans; tradesmen
 children as, 40–41, 61
 Chinese, 71, **71**
 "contract laborers," 70
 immigrants as, 15, 67
 Italians as, 51, **51**
 Jews as, 60
World War I, 74, **75**, 76

JAMES LINCOLN COLLIER is the author of a number of books both for adults and for young people, including the social history *The Rise of Selfishness in America*. He is also noted for his biographies and historical studies in the field of jazz. Together with his brother, Christopher Collier, he has written a series of award-winning historical novels for children widely used in schools, including the Newbery Honor classic, *My Brother Sam Is Dead*. A graduate of Hamilton College, he lives with his wife in New York City.

CHRISTOPHER COLLIER grew up in Fairfield County, Connecticut and attended public schools there. He graduated from Clark University in Worcester, Massachusetts and earned M.A. and Ph.D. degrees at Columbia University in New York City. After service in the Army and teaching in secondary schools for several years, Mr. Collier began teaching college in 1961. He is now Professor of History at the University of Connecticut and Connecticut State Historian. Mr. Collier has published many scholarly and popular books and articles about Connecticut and American history. With his brother, James, he is the author of nine historical novels for young adults, the best known of which is *My Brother Sam Is Dead*. He lives with his wife Bonnie, a librarian, in Orange, Connecticut.